Listen Up!

How to Hear the Voice of God

Advantage INSPIRATIONAL

Michael Janiczek

To God the Father, Who created all things

To my Lord and Savior, Jesus Christ, Who paid the ultimate price for my salvation

To the Holy Spirit, Who lives in me and empowers me to carry out God's plan for my life

To my wife, Karen, who has always prayed for me and believed in me when seemingly no one else did

And to our children, Tiffany, Heather and David, who are blessings to us

Michael Janiczek

Acknowledgements

I must acknowledge Norvel Hayes and New Life Bible College for the rock solid foundation I have in the Word of God.

Finis Jennings Dake for the insight he gave me into the scriptures, both in person as well as through his prolific writings.

Special thanks to Dr. Gary Barkman and Dayspring Christian University.

Many great men and woman of God have teamed with, worked and ministered with me and my wife, Karen throughout the years. All of those life experiences, good and bad, have molded me into the person that I am today.

Michael Janiczek

Table of Contents

Michael Janiczek

Preface

I have been a Christian most of my life. I am a Bible College graduate, and have been married over 32 years. My wife Karen and I have three wonderful children. I have worked in Christian publishing for more than 23 years.

I am just like you - no different. I am going through life doing the things that I think are right, making decisions for myself and my family that I think is the right things. Life has had its ups and downs, both in my personal and business life, but I have worked hard and succeeded. All in all, I would say that I have had a successful life.

Except in one area. Until recently, I had not had an ongoing communication with God. I was not communicating regularly with Him and as far as I knew, He was not communicating with me.

I WAS WRONG!

Even though we had graduated from Bible College and were eligible to be ordained into the ministry, my wife and I had chosen to remain lay ministers. We decided to be workers in the church. Over the years, whatever church we attended, we worked as volunteers in various ministries: music, worship, drama, children's, youth, young adult ministry, and as small group leaders. Wherever there was a need, we would jump in.

Because of opportunities that became available to us in the area of drama and music, we decided to attain our ordination through our school, New Life Bible College, which we had attended. During the ordination service, they imparted to us a calling as ministers of the Gospel. Both Dr. Norvel Hayes and Dr. Christian Harfouche prophesied over us and over our children.

While Dr. Harfouche was preaching, he stopped and called me forward. He was impressed by God to pray for my hearing. He said that my hearing was lacking and he laid hands on my left ear and prayed that God would open my ears. I did not have a hearing problem that I could discern, so I did not feel or hear anything differently at that moment.

However, what did happen was amazing to me. That night on the drive home God started to talk to me, and He has not stopped talking to me since. From that night on until today, I have heard God speak to me every day. My spiritual ears were opened. Now that I know His voice, I have come to realize that He has been talking to me all along - not only when I ask for something in prayer, but all of the time. I just had not been listening.

The voice of God is not always evident to us, yet it is easily seen. It is not always audible, yet it is easily heard. Is it not always recognized, but it is easily understood. These statements seem like opposites. How can something not be evident but easily seen, not be audible but easily heard, not be recognized but easily understood?

Listen up, because I will do my best to explain, as I tell you my story in the pages ahead.

Michael Janiczek

Chapter One

God Desires Communication with Us!

God created man to have fellowship.

According to His Word, God created mankind in order to have fellowship with them. He wanted fellowship, someone to talk to. According to the book of Genesis, God walked and talked with Adam and Eve in the Garden of Eden. He had one-on-one communication with them.

This was His plan from the beginning. Satan foiled that plan and ruined the intimate relationship that man had with God. Of course, God, Who is omniscient (all-knowing) and omnipresent (everywhere at the same time), knew this would happen. Before the foundation of the earth, God had prepared the plan of salvation.

³Blessed be the God and Father of our Lord Jesus Christ, who hath blessed us with all spiritual blessings in heavenly places in Christ: ⁴According as he hath chosen us in him before the foundation of the world, that *we should be holy and without blame before him in love: ⁵Having predestinated us unto the adoption of children by Jesus Christ to himself, according to the good pleasure of his will, ⁶To the praise of the glory of his grace, wherein he hath made us accepted in the beloved. (Ephesians 1:3-6)*

He has always desired communication with me.

For the first thirty-two years of my walk with God (until the age of fifty), it was hard for me to understand that God wanted to talk with me. However, once my ears were opened and I began to hear Him speak, I also noticed that not only does He desire me to talk to Him, He was trying to communicate with me. I realized that He had been communicating with me all along. The problem was I did not always hear. I was not always listening. When I did hear something, I did not always recognize that it was God.

I was born and raised in a Catholic family from the South Side of Chicago. While we were very religious, (religious being the key word here) I did not have a personal relationship with Jesus until the age of eighteen, when I accepted Jesus Christ as the Lord and Savior of my life.

Yes, we went to church, and did all the good Catholic things, but there was no relationship with Jesus. I could not have found a scripture verse to save my life. I was just going through the religious motions that every good Catholic boy did.

Even before my salvation experience, I always felt God in my life. I could not honestly say that I heard His voice, not in the sense of hearing an audible voice; however, I always had a sense that He was real and that there was some kind of call on my life.

Our family attended church every Sunday and I attended Catholic schools for most of my grammar school education. When we were not in Catholic schools, we would attend catechism classes called CCD that were designed to train us to become good Catholics.

Before my conversion experience, there was only one time that I had ever attended a church service outside of the Catholic Church. I was in the sixth grade and a neighborhood friend invited me to his youth group service. Anyone who attended with him would receive free passes to the roller rink. During the winter I would sometimes roller skate at a local rink on Saturdays. I was a good skater and it was fun to get out and spend the afternoon skating. Since this was an opportunity to get free passes, I decided to go along.

Little did I know what I was getting myself into! My friend was Baptist, and his church was holding revival meetings that week. This "free roller rink pass" campaign was an effort to get young people to attend their church and get saved. I remember laughing at the pastor's persistence during his altar call. He would exhort all sinners to walk the aisle; they would play a song and wait. As long as one person walked the aisle, he would give another call. This seemed to go on for at least thirty minutes. As I recall, several people got saved that night. I sat there uncomfortable and laughing at what was going on.

As I look back on that time now, I am grateful that God gave me another chance. He was calling me that night, but I did not know His voice. I rejected that call. Thank God I lived to have another chance!

Many years had passed, and by this time I had graduated from Harold L. Richards High School in Oak Lawn, Illinois. I was a good student and had developed a great interest in science and math. In fact, I had formed the opinion that God was not real and had adopted a belief in the theory of evolution.

My second chance at salvation came in the fall of 1975, right before I was to attend junior college. I had asked a girl out on a date. Her name was Karen Stone. She was a beautiful girl that I had known in high school. I took her out on a Saturday night and at the end of the date I asked her what she was doing tomorrow night (Sunday). She said that she was going to church. I asked her if I could go with her, and she said yes.

I picked her up the next evening and we drove to Homewood Full Gospel Church, which was about a 35-minute-drive from her home. On the way there, she said that her church was a full gospel church and that they danced in the aisle and spoke in tongues. I did not know what speaking in tongues was, so I just shrugged it off.

As we drove, I was debating Karen about God all the way to the church. All that I knew about evolution I spouted out to her. I was relentless in my efforts to declare that evolution was what I believed in.

When we arrived at the church and I walked in, I really felt something different there. I sat on the front row by myself (Karen had to sing in the choir) and what struck me the most was that everyone seemed to be happy. They were singing songs and yes, some actually did dance in the aisle. Some people spoke in tongues and there were interpretations in English of those tongues. It all seemed very strange to me; I did not know what was going on.

I had attended Catholic mass all my life. Those church services were solemn and dignified and any personal involvement was scripted for you in advance. Sit, stand, kneel; recite a few words here and there. It was all written out for us and the priest would direct the congregation along the way. The difference was like night and day. What was happening at this church could not have been more different from what I was used to.

The pastor at Homewood Full Gospel Church was Walter Peterson. After all the music and singing was over, he began to preach. I did not know what it was at the time, but God began communicating with me that night. Pastor Peterson seemed to know all about me. He was "reading my mail." As far as I was concerned, his message could have been titled "The Life and Times of Mike Janiczek."

After the service Pastor Peterson would greet everyone at the back door of the church.

When I got to the door he shook my hand and introduced himself and asked me if I knew Jesus as Lord and Savior of my life.

I said no and that I really believed in evolution.

Then he asked me if I had ever read the Bible.

I thought about it for a moment. Even though I was born and raised Catholic, I do not think I had ever opened a Bible to read it. So I answered him, "No, I have not ever read the Bible."

He said, "You probably have read a lot of books about evolution to come to believe in it. How can you make a decision about the reality of God if you do not read His Word?" He then handed me a Bible and challenged me to read it before I drew any conclusions about the reality of God.

Needless to say, I did read the Bible and it came alive to me. I kept attending church with Karen and every week the Pastor kept reading my mail, so much so that I accused Karen of communicating with the pastor each week about me. It never failed - each sermon was the life and times of Mike! You would think I would have got it quickly. In fact, it took several months to get through to me, but I finally made a decision to accept Jesus as Lord and Savior of my life. At that time I did not realize God was talking to me through that pastor and through His Word, but He was.

About a year later Karen and I were married. Six months later - in fact, it was on our six-month-anniversary - my mother-in-law called us and told us we needed to come and hear an evangelist that was in town. She told us that she had heard him and she had never heard anyone like him.

Karen and I decided to go that night and my mother-in-law was right. Norvel Hayes was the speaker and he was powerful. We attended several nights after that and made sure we were there on the front row each night. The power of God was strong and the message that he was delivering on faith was anointed.

The last night of the meetings, while sitting on the front row, I felt impressed to quit my job and go to Bible College. I don't remember hearing much of the message because I was overwhelmed at what God was telling me. I had never heard the voice of God and I was not sure that I knew what to do. It was like this idea was suddenly dropped in my mind. I really felt like this was something God wanted me to do. It was not a passing thought, but was more like a strong urge to go right now. I somehow knew that I needed to do this thing immediately.

I then realized that I was married and that Karen did not marry me thinking I was going to be a preacher. I spent the rest of that service squirming in my seat, worrying about how I would tell Karen and how she would react.

After the service ended, I turned to Karen and told her that I felt God wanted me to quit my job immediately and to attend Bible College. To my utter amazement, she replied, "I know. God told me the same thing tonight."

I was astonished! We stood there and hugged for a moment and then I realized what had just happened. We were both going to quit our jobs the next day and go to Bible College.

I then asked Karen what Bible College we should attend. God had clearly spoken to both of us; however, it seemed like we only had received part of the message. The only Bible College I knew about was the college that Pastor Petersen had attended in Washington State, called Washington Bible College. The only reason I had knowledge of this school was because he had mentioned it in some of his sermons.

When Karen answered my question with, "I don't know where we should go," I noticed that Norvel, who had left the sanctuary, was going back up onto the stage. As soon as she finished her answer, Norvel said, "I forgot to mention this all week, but I am starting a new Bible College this fall. If you know anyone who would like to attend, see me in the back."

It seemed like this was another answer from God. The teaching we received that week was tremendous and the thought of attending a Bible College with that sort of teaching was fantastic. Needless to say we went to the back of the room and spoke to the speaker about attending his Bible College.

Karen and I went on to attend that Bible College. I became the president of the first graduating class of New Life Bible College and it was a defining moment in our lives that came to pass after hearing God speak.

We listened and obeyed what God told us. We have received many blessings in our lives over the years, and I do believe that these blessings are the result of our obedience to His call. God spoke to both of us that night and this was just the beginning.

God knows all.

Of course, He knew all this would happen in advance, so all of these situations fell into place because He is an all-knowing God.

God has perfect knowledge of us - all our thoughts and all of our actions are open before him. The fact that God knows all things (is omniscient), and is everywhere, (is omnipresent), are biblical truths that are indisputable among Bible scholars. However, these facts are seldom acknowledged or believed by natural man.

God takes notice of every step we take, right and wrong. He knows what rules we walk by, what end we walk toward, what company we walk with. He sees what I do at all times; even when I am alone, He is there. He hears every word I speak and even knows every thought I think. Wherever I am, whatever I say and whatever I do, He knows.

[1]O LORD, thou hast searched me, and known me. [2]Thou knowest my downsitting and mine uprising, thou understandest my thought afar off. [3]Thou compassest my path and my lying down, and art acquainted with all my ways. [4]For there is not a word in my tongue, but, lo,

O LORD, thou knowest it altogether. [5]Thou hast beset me behind and before, and laid thine hand upon me. [6]Such knowledge is too wonderful for me; it is high, I cannot attain unto it. [7]Whither shall I go from thy spirit? or whither shall I flee from thy presence? [8]If I ascend up into heaven, thou art there: if I make my bed in hell, behold, thou art there. [9]If I take the wings of the morning, and dwell in the uttermost parts of the sea; [10]Even there shall thy hand lead me, and thy right hand shall hold me. [11]If I say, Surely the darkness shall cover me; even the night shall be light about me. [12]Yea, the darkness hideth not from thee; but the night shineth as the day: the darkness and the light are both alike to thee. [13]For thou hast possessed my reins: thou hast covered me in my mother's womb. [14]I will praise thee; for I am fearfully and wonderfully made: marvellous are thy works; and that my soul knoweth right well. [15]My substance was not hid from thee, when I was made in secret, and curiously wrought in the lowest parts of the earth. [16]Thine eyes did see my substance, yet being unperfect; and in thy book all my members were written, which in continuance were fashioned, when as yet there was none of them. [17]How precious also are thy thoughts unto me, O God! how great is the sum of them! (Ps 139:1-17)

He knows what I will do, even before I do it.

It does not mean that He forced me in any way to make the choices I did, He just knows the beginning and the ending, and therefore He knows the outcome before it happens.

> [8]*I am Alpha and Omega, the beginning and the ending, saith the Lord, which is, and which was, and which is to come, the Almighty. (Revelation 1:8)*

He does not do anything to change the outcome. The entire debate about predestination and preordination is really easy to understand.

He predestined and preordained that all who accept Jesus as being the only begotten Son of God, Who was born of a virgin, suffered and died on the cross, then on the third day rose from the dead and then later ascended into heaven to be seated at the right hand of the Father, would be saved.

> [9]*That if thou shalt confess with thy mouth the Lord Jesus, and shalt believe in thine heart that God hath raised him from the dead, thou shalt be saved. [10]For with the heart man believeth unto righteousness; and with the mouth confession is made unto salvation. (Romans 10:9-10)*

16For God so loved the world, that he gave his only begotten Son, that whosoever believeth in him should not perish, but have everlasting life. (John 3:16)

That is not to say that He chose who would accept Him, only that those who do accept Him would be saved and have eternal life. It is really that simple.

Now that I know His voice as I do, I realize that God has been trying to communicate with me all my life. Even before I accepted Him as Lord and Savior, while I was lost and on my way to hell, He was there, tugging at my heart and trying to get my attention. I am not anyone special and God is no respecter of persons.

34Then Peter opened his mouth, and said, Of a truth I perceive that God is no respecter of persons: (Acts 10:34)

Therefore, I believe this means that whatever He has done for me, He has done the same for you. Search your heart, think back to a time before you were saved. Can you identify a time when God spoke to you? If so, what did He say?

It is fascinating to me when I think back on the times God spoke to me, how I reacted and what ultimately happened. I am glad that I now have a personal relationship with God and that I know and recognize His voice.

You too can have that personal relationship with Jesus. If you do not know Him this way, all you have to do is repent. Repent of your sins, and ask God to come into your life and be the Lord of your life. It is that easy. He loves you so much that He sent His only begotten Son to be born of a virgin and then to die on the cross for our sins. That's right…your sins and mine. And all you have to do is to ask Him into your heart. Once you do that you are joint heirs with Him.

> [16]*The Spirit itself beareth witness with our spirit, that we are the children of God:* [17]*And if children, then heirs; heirs of God, and joint-heirs with Christ; if so be that we suffer with him, that we may be also glorified together.* [18]*For I reckon that the sufferings of this present time are not worthy to be compared with the glory which shall be revealed in us. (Romans 8:16-18)*

Michael Janiczek

Chapter Two

He Promises To Answer Our Prayers

There are many scriptures that teach us that God answers prayers. While this is a simple undisputed doctrine of the Bible, many if not most Christians do not take advantage of this amazing truth.

I was one of them.

I don't mean to say that I never prayed. I prayed at church all of the time. I prayed before every meal and I would pray when someone asked for prayer or when things were bad and I really needed help. God heard all of those prayers and I believe He answered every one of them. But I knew in my heart that I did not pray enough and that God wanted more from me. What more does He want?

He desires us to talk to Him. He wants to know what you need, what you want, and what you desire. It is hard to understand because according to the Bible, He is an all-knowing God. However, the Bible also says that He wants us to tell Him anyway. If we do obey Him in this area, He is quick to answer.

Recently I played a round of golf at a local golf course. After completing the round, I went straight home to a quick shower before going out with my wife to dinner. At that point I realized that my wallet was missing. The last time I had it in my possession was at the golf course. I immediately called and asked them to look around the clubhouse for it. They could not find it and said that no one had turned in a wallet.

I was really upset because not only were my driver's license and credit cards in the wallet, but I also had about $450.00 in cash in it. I was mad at myself for being careless. I knew I had the wallet when I went to the golf course, so I was pretty sure I had lost it there.

We decided to go back to the golf course and look around for it. On the way there we prayed that God would protect my wallet and see to it that it was returned intact and full of everything that was in it, including the cash. It seemed like a tall order. For all I knew, someone could have already found it, taken the cash and thrown it away. Nevertheless I chose to believe that God would answer my prayer.

When I arrived back at the golf course, the sun had set and darkness made it impossible to look around. My wife told me she thought it was on the golf course grass near the road, (which was what God was telling her). However, I was sure that I must have left it on my cart.

The next morning I retuned at dawn to look around, just in case I could find it lying on the ground somewhere. I did not find it, so I returned home. At noon my wife got a call from the golf pro at the course.

Someone found my wallet on the eighteenth hole on the green. The first group out on the golf course was finishing their round when they found it and they turned it in. Everything was there - my driver's license, credit cards and all of the cash. They said it was lying on the ground next to the road. It had been there over eighteen hours and then someone found it and returned it in full.

You can call it a coincidence if you want; I believe God answered my prayers and God was talking to Karen about where it was. Karen was listening to the voice of God. And we both believed that my wallet would be returned intact. That was our faith at work.

There are many scriptures in the Bible that teach us this principle. If you are familiar with the Bible at all, you have read one or all of these scriptures; these are only a few of them.

> *Therefore I say unto you, What things soever ye desire, when ye pray, believe that ye receive them, and ye shall have them.*
> *(Mark 11:24)*

> *If ye abide in me, and my words abide in you, ye shall ask what ye will, and it shall be done unto you. (John 15:7)*

> *Ye have not chosen me, but I have chosen you, and ordained you, that ye should go and bring forth fruit, and that your fruit should remain:*

that whatsoever ye shall ask of the Father in my name, he may give it you. (John 15:16)

Why is it so hard for us to understand this biblical truth? God clearly tells us we can ask Him for anything, and as long as we ask in the Name of Jesus, believe and not doubt, and if we abide in Him and His Word abides in us, then whatever we desire, whatever we ask for, He will see to it that we receive it.

When we ask the Father anything in Jesus' Name, He hears and answers our prayers.

As Christians, you would think we would take full advantage of these promises. If we did, we would have no needs. We could go about His work and spread the gospel in all the earth.

In fact, I am convinced this is the reason He made such an amazing promise to give us whatever we need, want or desire. It was so we can fulfill His great commission: to spread the gospel over all the earth. How else could any of us expect to fulfill this command?

Sadly, for most of my life, even though I was a Christian, I did not have daily communication with the Father. In fact, I had gotten to a point in my life where I did not read the Bible much anymore. So I had reached a point where I did not qualify to receive answered prayer. Whose fault was that? Mine!

Therefore, when I struggled or had a need, I did not even ask. Since I did not ask, I did not receive.

And I say unto you, Ask, and it shall be given you; seek, and ye shall find; knock, and it shall be opened unto you. (Luke 11:9)

In fact, I did not qualify for my prayers to be answered. I was not abiding in the vine, and His Words were not in me. Who was to blame? I was!

I had become a desperate prayer. I only prayed when things became critical. I have to admit that during most of our married life my wife took the leadership role in the area of prayer in our family. As I said, other than praying for meals and the occasional bedtime prayer with the children, I did not pray very much. I could not ever seem to get into a daily routine where prayer was concerned. I knew it was a problem, but I could not seem to do anything about it. I was always too busy. I did not have the time to spend with God. But in fact, that was just an excuse. I could find the time for anything that was a priority. That was the problem; prayer was not a priority in my life.

This is not intended to be a book about prayer, but it is one of the byproducts that came to me after I began to hear God more clearly.

From the time my ears were opened and I began to hear God clearly, I became so "on fire" for God that I could not get enough. Karen and I now begin each day with devotions and prayer. Sometimes we even do devotions two or more times a day. The more we study His word and pray, the more He speaks to us.

I do not think this has anything to do with God changing His ways; rather that I have finally tuned in to His voice and can recognize when He speaks and what He is saying.

Hearing God's voice was not easy for me at first. I am not saying I could not easily hear Him, but because of the great emotions it stirred in me it was a bit embarrassing for me, as a man, to get that emotional in front of others. You see, when God speaks to me I get very emotional, to the point where I begin crying out loud. This is not a problem while I am in my prayer closet at home or even when I am in devotions with my family and friends. But God began speaking to me each and every day at different times throughout the day.

I might be doing a chore like cutting the lawn, or perhaps driving the car, or while in the grocery store or in a restaurant or at a movie.

Recently I was doing lawn work out in front of my home when the Spirit of the Lord came upon me. He began telling me an answer to a specific prayer that I had prayed. I began to cry, but did not stop what I was doing. God did not stop talking to me, and I did not stop working and crying. Unbeknownst to me, my neighbor was walking her dog on the street and observed me crying like a baby while pushing my lawn mower. The next thing I knew she came up to me. I stopped the lawn mower so I could hear her. She asked me if something was wrong. I said no, that I was fine and that God was talking to me.

Needless to say, she probably thinks I am crazy. I did not want to lie to her, so I just told her God was blessing me at that moment. She looked at me and smiled. She went on walking her dog and I went on cutting my lawn. I had told her the truth about what was happening.

When I was growing up, my father would hit us if we cried. He said that men did not cry. So, with that instilled in me, I had a hard time with this manifestation I wanted not to exude emotion while God was talking to me. However, I have come to grips with the fact that I react to His voice this way and that it is a blessing and I am not ashamed of it. Many times it happens at times and in places where you might least expect it to happen.

Recently I was at a concert at Stetson University, where my daughter Heather was a student. She was a music major at the time and we would attend various concerts. At this particular concert there was a mix of instrumentalists and vocalists performing that night in a very quaint music hall that seats about 350 people. The etiquette for concerts of this type is that the audience sits quietly and only applauds at specific times when a performance is completed.

In the middle of this concert, God began to talk to me and I began to cry. I was trying to control myself so as not to make a scene or disturb the young lady who was performing on a violin. She was looking right at me and she must have thought that either I really liked or really hated what she was playing.

Little did she know that God was speaking to me about the beauty that He sees in certain things. He said to me, "I find that beautiful." He told me that man picks the most beautiful, handsome, popular, smart or athletic people and holds them in high esteem. But He told me that he looks at the heart of a person and what is inside - that is what really matters, not outward appearances. This is something I knew about God. However, He chose that moment to show me this fact in a new way.

I have learned not to be ashamed of the way I react when God speaks to me. While driving to my daughter's college graduation with my wife and her parents, God started to talk to me again and I started to weep. My mother-in-law turned to Karen and said, "Mike is crying." Karen's response to that was, "He does that all the time when God talks to him."

No matter when He speaks to me, I listen. Most of the time it is in private, but even when it is in public, I have learned to listen to what He is saying and not to worry what others may think about my outward reaction.

What I have learned is that God wants us to tell Him everything. It is a form of obedience that really is very simple. Why don't you try it for yourself? Tell Him about your troubles, fears, needs and desires and watch what happens. He will answer every prayer. He guarantees it in His Word.

Chapter Three

How Does God Communicate With Man?

Does your VCR blink 12:00AM?

Back in the 1970's when VCR's (Video Cassette Recorders) first came out, I had a friend who never learned how to program his VCR. Every time I went over to his home I would see their VCR clock blinking 12:00 AM, which indicated the VCR was not properly programmed. He never read the owner's manual and even though I would tell him how to fix it, he did not understand it. In those days, most people did not understand how to use a VCR. You had to read the manual in order to properly use one.

Now in the twenty-first century we have DVR's (Digital Video Recorders) that are virtually self - explanatory compared to what our parents had (the VCR's). Today's generation does not understand what we went through setting up the original programming on VCR's just to get the clock to work, not to mention setting the correct time to start and end recording, as well as making the connections that were needed just to receive a signal.

Much like humans, the original VCR began as a blank canvas. It had to be programmed by the owner to learn everything. It was not at all tied to a clock, or to the television schedule, for that matter. The owner had to program it to know what the correct current time and day was, so that you could tell the VCR when to begin and end recording during the week. The VCR also had its own television tuner that you had to connect to your antenna or cable in order to record the channels that your television received.

The VCR recorded on tapes that could hold two, four or six hours, depending on the recording speed that you chose. All of this required the owner to read the manual in order to set up the VCR. If you did not set it up correctly, your VCR clock would eternally blink 12:00AM.

In some respects, we humans are the same. We begin as a blank canvas. Yes, I know that there is genetic programming, as well as certain instincts we have, but for the sake of this example, let's assume we are all blank canvases. The owner's manual is the Bible. God has printed in it everything we need to know including information on who we really are, how to act, what to say, how to prosper and be in health, how to become and stay successful, as well as the keys to the kingdom.

Yet most Christians have not even read the manual. They are like my friend; they listen to their preacher and he tells them how to format their lives, instead of reading the owner's manual for themselves. Therefore they are not properly programmed, and if there was such an indicator (like the VCR clock) on Christians who are not programmed on how to act, how to talk, how to be a Christian, I am convinced that most "Christian Clocks" would blink 12:00 AM, because they have no clue. They have never read the owner's manual (the Bible) and therefore do not act anything like a Christian.

The number one way to get to know God and to learn how to act in every situation is through the Bible, which is His Word.

[1]In the beginning was the Word, and the Word was with God, and the Word was God.
(John 1:1)

We seem to forget that every word recorded in the Bible is God's Word. Like an owner's manual for a car, the Bible is a handbook for living. The funny thing about owner's manuals is that most people do not read them - much like my friend with his VCR!

We should pick up our owner's manual, which is the Bible, and study it and learn from it. It truly is a handbook for living.

[11]These were more noble than those in Thessalonica, in that they received the word with all readiness of mind, and searched the scriptures daily, whether those things were so. (Acts 17:11)

Let's look to the Bible to see how God communicates with man. Look at these scriptures:

The angel of the Lord appeared to Moses out of a burning bush and spoke to him in an audible voice. It was a message spoken out loud:

[2]And the angel of the LORD appeared unto him in a flame of fire out of the midst of a bush: and he looked, and, behold, the bush burned with fire, and the bush was not consumed [3]And Moses said, I will now turn aside, and see this great sight, why the bush is not burnt. [4]And when the LORD saw that he turned aside to see, God called unto him out of the midst of the bush, and said, Moses, Moses. And he said, Here am I. 5And he said, Draw not nigh hither: put off thy shoes from off thy feet, for the place whereon thou standest is holy ground. (Exodus 3:2-5)

God was talking to Moses out of a cloud in public in an audible voice for all to hear.

²⁵And the LORD came down in a cloud, and spake unto him, and took of the spirit that was upon him, and gave it unto the seventy elders: and it came to pass, that, when the spirit rested upon them, they prophesied, and did not cease. (Numbers 11:25)

God talked to Noah out in the open in. an audible voice:

¹³And God said unto Noah, The end of all flesh is come before me; for the earth is filled with violence through them; and, behold, I will destroy them with the earth. ¹⁴Make thee an ark of gopher wood; rooms shalt thou make in the ark, and shalt pitch it within and without with pitch. ¹⁵And this is the fashion which thou shalt make it of: The length of the ark shall be three hundred cubits, the breadth of it fifty cubits, and the height of it thirty cubits. ¹⁶A window shalt thou make to the ark, and in a cubit shalt thou finish it above; and the door of the ark shalt thou set in the side thereof; with lower, second, and third stories shalt thou make it. ¹⁷And, behold, I, even I, do bring a flood of waters upon the earth, to destroy all flesh, wherein is the breath of life, from under heaven; and every thing that is in the earth shall die. ¹⁸But with thee will I establish my covenant; and thou

shalt come into the ark, thou, and thy sons, and thy wife, and thy sons' wives with thee. (Genesis 6:13-18)

God appeared in a vision to Abram (Abraham) and spoke directly to him in an audible voice:

¹After these things the word of the LORD came unto Abram in a vision, saying, Fear not, Abram: I am thy shield, and thy exceeding great reward. (Genesis 15:1)

What do you see in common? Before the Holy Spirit was given to men after the death and resurrection of Christ, God had to send angels in person as messengers, or speak audibly out loud, as He did with Moses, Abraham or at Jesus' baptism.

I used to think it would be cool to hear God's voice out loud like that; however, I am convinced it does not happen that way any more.

All of the scriptures that record an audible voice spoken out for all to hear happened before the Holy Spirit was sent to dwell in us.

Now that He (the Holy Spirit) lives in me, God has a direct internal point of contact, which He uses to communicate directly to each individual Christian.

What's that baggage you're handling?

God did create man to have fellowship with Him, but sin caused a temporary break in the lines of communication. The original sin was the sin of Adam and Eve in the Garden of Eden.

> *[7]And the LORD God formed man of the dust of the ground, and breathed into his nostrils the breath of life; and man became a living soul. [8]And the LORD God planted a garden eastward in Eden; and there he put the man whom he had formed. [9]And out of the ground made the LORD God to grow every tree that is pleasant to the sight, and good for food; the tree of life also in the midst of the garden, and the tree of knowledge of good and evil. (Genesis 2:7-9)*

> *[15]And the LORD God took the man, and put him into the garden of Eden to dress it and to keep it. [16]And the LORD God commanded the man, saying, Of every tree of the garden thou mayest freely eat: [17]But of the tree of the knowledge of good and evil, thou shalt not eat of it: for in the day that thou eatest thereof thou shalt surely die. (Genesis 2:15-17)*

God created man and set him in the Garden of Eden, which was a paradise that contained everything he needed. There was just one rule. Do not eat of the tree of the knowledge of good and evil.

[1]Now the serpent was more subtil than any beast of the field which the LORD God had made. And he said unto the woman, Yea, hath God said, Ye shall not eat of every tree of the garden? [2]And the woman said unto the serpent, We may eat of the fruit of the trees of the garden: [3]But of the fruit of the tree which is in the midst of the garden, God hath said, Ye shall not eat of it, neither shall ye touch it, lest ye die. [4]And the serpent said unto the woman, Ye shall not surely die: [5]For God doth know that in the day ye eat thereof, then your eyes shall be opened, and ye shall be as gods, knowing good and evil. [6]And when the woman saw that the tree was good for food, and that it was pleasant to the eyes, and a tree to be desired to make one wise, she took of the fruit thereof, and did eat, and gave also unto her husband with her; and he did eat. [7]And the eyes of them both were opened, and they knew that they were naked; and they sewed fig leaves together, and made themselves aprons. [8]And they heard the voice of the LORD God walking in the garden in the cool of the day: and Adam and his wife hid themselves from the presence of the LORD God amongst the trees of the garden. (Genesis 3:1-8)

[9]And the LORD God called unto Adam, and said unto him, Where art thou? [10]And he said,

I heard thy voice in the garden, and I was afraid, because I was naked; and I hid myself. ¹¹*And he said, Who told thee that thou wast naked? Hast thou eaten of the tree, whereof I commanded thee that thou shouldest not eat?* ¹²*And the man said, The woman whom thou gavest to be with me, she gave me of the tree, and I did eat.* ¹³*And the LORD God said unto the woman, What is this that thou hast done? And the woman said, The serpent beguiled me, and I did eat.* ¹⁴*And the LORD God said unto the serpent, Because thou hast done this, thou art cursed above all cattle, and above every beast of the field; upon thy belly shalt thou go, and dust shalt thou eat all the days of thy life:* ¹⁵*And I will put enmity between thee and the woman, and between thy seed and her seed; it shall bruise thy head, and thou shalt bruise his heel.* ¹⁶*Unto the woman he said, I will greatly multiply thy sorrow and thy conception; in sorrow thou shalt bring forth children; and thy desire shall be to thy husband, and he shall rule over thee.* ¹⁷*And unto Adam he said, Because thou hast hearkened unto the voice of thy wife, and hast eaten of the tree, of which I commanded thee, saying, Thou shalt not eat of it: cursed is the ground for thy sake; in sorrow shalt thou eat of it all the days of thy life;* ¹⁸*Thorns also and thistles shall it bring forth to thee; and thou shalt eat the herb of the field; [19]In the sweat of thy face shalt thou eat bread, till thou return unto the ground; for out of it wast thou taken: for dust thou art, and unto dust shalt thou return. [20]And Adam called his wife's name Eve; because she was the mother of all living. [21]Unto Adam also and to his wife did the LORD God make coats of skins, and clothed them. [22]And the LORD God said, Behold, the man is become as one of us, to know good and evil: and now, lest he put forth his hand, and take also of the tree of life, and eat, and live for ever: [23]Therefore the LORD God sent him forth from the garden of Eden, to till the ground from whence he was taken. [24]So he drove out the man; and he placed at the east of the garden of Eden Cherubims, and a flaming sword which turned every way, to keep the way of the tree of life. (Genesis 3:9-24)*

The original sin is what caused a break in man's lines of communication with God. God cannot be associated with sin. Even when He sent His Son to the cross as a sacrifice for our sin, He had to turn away from Jesus, because He had become sin for us.

[20]Now then we are ambassadors for Christ, as though God did beseech you by us: we pray you in Christ's stead, be ye reconciled to God. [21]For he hath made him to be sin for us, who

knew no sin; that we might be made the righteousness of God in him. (2 Corinthians 5:20-21)

[34]*And at the ninth hour Jesus cried with a loud voice, saying, Eloi, Eloi, lama sabachthani? which is, being interpreted, My God, my God, why hast thou forsaken me? (Mark 15:34)*

That word "forsaken" can be translated abandoned. Jesus, for the first time, felt what it was like to have communication with the Father broken because of sin.

Even though the lines of communication have been restored, most Christians unfortunately fail to utilize the reconnection.

Therefore (back to the time before restored communication), because of the original sin that had yet to be dealt with, God had to speak out loud in a voice projected out for all to hear. The Holy Spirit had not yet come to dwell in man; therefore, God had to speak outwardly in a voice that could be heard by all to communicate with man. God had no direct communication link with His creation.

Now that we have the Holy Spirit dwelling in us, God speaks directly to the heart of man. The Bible calls it being led by the Spirit.

¹And Jesus being full of the Holy Ghost returned from Jordan, and was led by the Spirit into the wilderness, (Luke 4:1)

¹⁴For as many as are led by the Spirit of God, they are the sons of God. (Romans 8:14)

¹⁶This I say then, Walk in the Spirit, and ye shall not fulfill the lust of the flesh. (Galatians 5:16)

¹⁸But if ye be led of the Spirit, ye are not under the law.(Galatians 5:18)

Having the means of communication available is not enough.

God has done His part. By sending His Son Jesus as a perfect sacrifice for our sins, and then sending the Holy Spirit to dwell in us as our Comforter, God has restored the lines of communication with man.

However, because God desires fellowship with us that is pure and real, we have to <u>choose</u> Him. He will not force us to accept Him.

At the same time, the devil has been defeated but he is still here to tempt us. He has no power left and we have been given dominion over all sin and temptation.

God describes it for us in Romans, Chapters seven and eight. Let's take time to go over it verse by verse. If you will take the time to study this and receive God's wisdom from these few verses, it will change your life!

Beginning in verse five of Chapter seven in Romans, God describes the difference between following your flesh or His Spirit.

> *⁵For when we were in the flesh, the motions of sins, which were by the law, did work in our members to bring forth fruit unto death. (Romans 7:5)*

Simply stated, this says that the result of following the desires of the flesh is sin. As revealed by the law, sin leads to death.

> *⁶But now we are delivered from the law, that being dead wherein we were held; that we should serve in newness of spirit, and not in the oldness of the letter. ⁷What shall we say then? Is the law sin? God forbid. Nay, I had not known sin, but by the law: for I had not known lust, except the law had said, Thou shalt not covet. ⁸But sin, taking occasion by the commandment, wrought in me all manner of concupiscence. For without the law sin was dead. (Romans 7:6-8)*

God says here that the Old Testament law, given to Moses, was sent to reveal man's sin, and without the law sin did not exist.

⁹For I was alive without the law once: but when the commandment came, sin revived, and I died. ¹⁰And the commandment, which was ordained to life, I found to be unto death. ¹¹For sin, taking occasion by the commandment, deceived me, and by it slew me. ¹²Wherefore the law is holy, and the commandment holy, and just, and good. ¹³Was then that which is good made death unto me? God forbid. But sin, that it might appear sin, working death in me by that which is good; that sin by the commandment might become exceeding sinful. ¹⁴For we know that the law is spiritual: but I am carnal, sold under sin. (Romans 7:9-14)

Here Paul is saying he was alive before he understood the law, but when he came to understand the law, sin became alive in him. He goes on to say that the commandments were meant to bring life, but because of the sin that dwells in him (a remnant of the original sin) the commandment (or laws) revealed the sin working in him and therefore brought death.

Here is how…

¹⁵For that which I do I allow not: for what I would, that do I not; but what I hate, that do I. ¹⁶If then I do that which I would not, I consent unto the law that it is good. ¹⁷Now then it is no more I that do it, but sin that dwelleth in me.

¹⁸For I know that in me (that is, in my flesh,) dwelleth no good thing: for to will is present with me; but how to perform that which is good I find not. ¹⁹For the good that I would I do not: but the evil which I would not, that I do. ²⁰Now if I do that I would not, it is no more I that do it, but sin that dwelleth in me. ²¹I find then a law, that, when I would do good, evil is present with me. ²²For I delight in the law of God after the inward man: ²³But I see another law in my members, warring against the law of my mind, and bringing me into captivity to the law of sin which is in my members. (Romans 7:15-23)

Basically these scriptures explain why we all fail. The things that we know we should not do, we do, and the things we know we should do, we don't do. This internal war affects all of us and is caused by the remnant of the original sin

²⁴O wretched man that I am! Who shall deliver me from the body of this death? ²⁵I thank God through Jesus Christ our Lord. So then with the mind I myself serve the law of God; but with the flesh the law of sin. (Romans 7:24-25)

The only way to win this battle is to accept Jesus Christ as Lord and Savior and abide in Him. Chapter eight of Romans goes on to explain more.

> *[1]There is therefore now no condemnation to them which are in Christ Jesus, who walk not after the flesh, but after the Spirit. [2]For the law of the Spirit of life in Christ Jesus hath made me free from the law of sin and death. (Romans 8:1-2)*

We are no longer condemned by the original sin, because the Law of the Spirit has set us free.

Make no mistake; all the sins that we commit have been dealt with by Jesus' death and resurrection. We need to ask for forgiveness and accept the fact that Jesus paid the price for our sins.

But it is the original sin of Adam and Eve he is talking about here. That is still present because it was not removed, though it has been condemned.

> *[3]For what the law could not do, in that it was weak through the flesh, God sending his own Son in the likeness of sinful flesh, and for sin, condemned sin in the flesh: (Romans 8:3)*

The reason we do the things we know we should not do, as stated in Chapter seven, is because that thing that gnaws at you from the inside, those evil thoughts that you still have to deal with, those come from the remnant of the original sin.

You see, the original sin is still present. It has been dealt with separately and in a different way. This sin God has condemned, but not removed.

What does this mean?

It is like an empty cardboard box that is thrown into a fire. Before being consumed by the fire, that box could be filled with maybe 50 or 60 pounds of contents and then be picked up and carried away. After being consumed by the fire, the cardboard box keeps its original shape; however, its strength is gone. If you try to pick it up, it dissolves into ashes.

Having been condemned by God, this original sin (or sin of the flesh) has been stripped of its power and control over us. We have been exonerated, or liberated from its power. In other words, God judged original sin and pronounced it to be unfit for use or service to believers.

This is huge! This original sin has no more power over us as long as we walk in the Spirit!

[4]That the righteousness of the law might be fulfilled in us, who walk not after the flesh, but after the Spirit. [5]For they that are after the flesh do mind the things of the flesh; but they that are after the Spirit the things of the Spirit. [6]For to be carnally minded is death; but to be spiritually minded is life and peace. [7]Because the carnal mind is enmity against God: for it

is not subject to the law of God, neither indeed can be. [8]So then they that are in the flesh cannot please God. [9]But ye are not in the flesh, but in the Spirit, if so be that the Spirit of God dwell in you. Now if any man have not the Spirit of Christ, he is none of his. [10]And if Christ be in you, the body is dead because of sin; but the Spirit is life because of righteousness. [11]But if the Spirit of him that raised up Jesus from the dead dwell in you, he that raised up Christ from the dead shall also quicken your mortal bodies by his Spirit that dwelleth in you. (Romans 8: 4-11)

That is why God pronounces that we are more than conquerors! We are not just warriors; we are victors. In fact we are more than victors, we are more than conquerors. We are heirs, joint-heirs with Jesus!

[12]Therefore, brethren, we are debtors, not to the flesh, to live after the flesh. [13]For if ye live after the flesh, ye shall die: but if ye through the Spirit do mortify the deeds of the body, ye shall live. [14]For as many as are led by the Spirit of God, they are the sons of God. [15]For ye have not received the spirit of bondage again to fear; but ye have received the Spirit of adoption, whereby we cry, Abba, Father. [16]The Spirit itself beareth witness with our spirit, that we are the children of God: [17]And

if children, then heirs; heirs of God, and joint-heirs with Christ; if so be that we suffer with him, that we may be also glorified together. ¹⁸*For I reckon that the sufferings of this present time are not worthy to be compared with the glory which shall be revealed in us.* ¹⁹*For the earnest expectation of the creature waiteth for the manifestation of the sons of God.* ²⁰*For the creature was made subject to vanity, not willingly, but by reason of him who hath subjected the same in hope,* ²¹*Because the creature itself also shall be delivered from the bondage of corruption into the glorious liberty of the children of God.* ²²*For we know that the whole creation groaneth and travaileth in pain together until now.* ²³*And not only they, but ourselves also, which have the firstfruits of the Spirit, even we ourselves groan within ourselves, waiting for the adoption, to wit, the redemption of our body.* ²⁴*For we are saved by hope: but hope that is seen is not hope: for what a man seeth, why doth he yet hope for?* ²⁵*But if we hope for that we see not, then do we with patience wait for it.* ²⁶*Likewise the Spirit also helpeth our infirmities: for we know not what we should pray for as we ought: but the Spirit itself maketh intercession for us with groanings which cannot be uttered.* ²⁷*And he that searcheth the hearts knoweth what is the mind* of the Spirit, because he maketh intercession for the saints according to the will of God. ²⁸And we know that all things work together for good to them that love God, to them who are the called according to his purpose. ²⁹For whom he did foreknow, he also did predestinate to be conformed to the image of his Son, that he might be the firstborn among many brethren. ³⁰Moreover whom he did predestinate, them he also called: and whom he called, them he also justified: and whom he justified, them he also glorified. ³¹What shall we then say to these things? If God be for us, who can be against us? ³²He that spared not his own Son, but delivered him up for us all, how shall he not with him also freely give us all things? ³³Who shall lay any thing to the charge of God's elect? It is God that justifieth. ³⁴Who is he that condemneth? It is Christ that died, yea rather, that is risen again, who is even at the right hand of God, who also maketh intercession for us. ³⁵Who shall separate us from the love of Christ? shall tribulation, or distress, or persecution, or famine, or nakedness, or peril, or sword? ³⁶As it is written, For thy sake we are killed all the day long; we are accounted as sheep for the slaughter. ³⁷Nay, in all these things we are more than conquerors through him that loved us. ³⁸For I am persuaded, that neither death, *nor life, nor angels, nor principalities, nor powers, nor things present, nor things to come, [39]Nor height, nor depth, nor any other creature, shall be able to separate us from the love of God, which is in Christ Jesus our Lord. (Romans 8:12-39)*

In fact, when the Holy Spirit came to dwell in you, He brought with Him gifts. He distributes these gifts of the Spirit as He sees fit. Think of them as housewarming gifts that you might bring to a friend's home when you come to visit for the first time.

[4]Now there are diversities of gifts, but the same Spirit. [5]And there are differences of administrations, but the same Lord. [6]And there are diversities of operations, but it is the same God which worketh all in all. [7]But the manifestation of the Spirit is given to every man to profit withal. [8]For to one is given by the Spirit the word of wisdom; to another the word of knowledge by the same Spirit; [9]To another faith by the same Spirit; to another the gifts of healing by the same Spirit; [10]To another the working of miracles; to another prophecy; to another discerning of spirits; to another divers kinds of tongues; to another the interpretation of tongues: [11]But all these worketh that one and the selfsame Spirit,

dividing to every man severally as he will. (1 Corinthians 12:4-11)

The Holy Spirit wants to give you gifts. In fact we are told to seek after them.

[30]Have all the gifts of healing? do all speak with tongues? do all interpret? [31]But covet earnestly the best gifts: and yet shew I unto you a more excellent way.
(1 Corinthians 12:30-31)

That phrase in verse 31 (to covet) actually means "to truly want" or "to desire." Therefore, the Holy Spirit wants you to want His gifts, to seek after them, to ask Him for them. Have you ever asked the Holy Spirit for any gifts?

[9]And I say unto you, Ask, and it shall be given you; seek, and ye shall find; knock, and it shall be opened unto you. [10]For every one that asketh receiveth; and he that seeketh findeth; and to him that knocketh it shall be opened.
(Luke 11:9-10)

It is by the Spirit that you can hear God's voice inside you. In addition, the Bible tells us to ask for wisdom. And notice that three of the gifts of the Spirit are revelation gifts that God <u>communicates</u> to us: the word of wisdom, the word of knowledge, and discerning of spirits.

> *[19]What? know ye not that your body is the temple of the Holy Ghost which is in you, which ye have of God, and ye are not your own? (1 Corinthians 6:19)*

> *[28]For in him we live, and move, and have our being... (Acts 17:28)*

Therefore, we can conclude that if you are born again, the Holy Spirit of God dwells in you, and that you live in Christ. With this knowledge, I have one question. What is it that you face that you cannot overcome? What situation in your life troubles you to the point where you have almost given up?

Trust God! Only Believe! With God all things are possible!

Our job is twofold: believe and do not doubt!

> *[22]And Jesus answering saith unto them, Have faith in God. [23]For verily I say unto you, That whosoever shall say unto this mountain, Be thou removed, and be thou cast into the sea; and shall not doubt in his heart, but shall believe that those things which he saith shall come to pass; he shall have whatsoever he saith. [24]Therefore I say unto you, What things*

*soever ye desire, when ye pray, believe that ye
receive them, and ye shall have them.*
(Mark 11:22-24)

I think that most Christians think they have only
one job, to believe, but the scriptures are clear there are
two parts to receiving what you need from God.

1) Believe
2) Do not doubt.

Do you find yourself in a situation where you have
not received from God? Do a quick check. If you are
honest, I believe that you will find that either you did
not believe what you prayed, or you doubted it. There is
a difference between believing and not doubting. You
must do both to meet the scriptural qualifications to
receive your prayers answered from God.

God has a direct internal link to all those that know
Him.

This clears up another point that some Christians
argue about. Do those believers who are not baptized in
the Holy Ghost have the Holy Spirit in them? The
answer is yes. Here is what the Bible says:

*[1]And it came to pass, that, while Apollos was
at Corinth, Paul having passed through the
upper coasts came to Ephesus: and finding
certain disciples, [2a]He said unto them, Have*

ye received the Holy Ghost since ye believed?
(Acts 19:1-2a)

You see, Paul asked the disciples at Ephesus if they had received the baptism of the Holy Ghost as yet. They were disciples (believers in Christ) so he knew that they already had the Holy Spirit dwelling in them (the same Spirit that raised Christ from the dead dwells in you), but they had not yet received the baptism of the Holy Ghost, which comes with the evidence of speaking in tongues.

There are many ways that God speaks to us. Here is a list of the ways that God speaks to New Testament believers:

1　Through His Word
2　By the Inspiration of the Holy Spirit:
3　Visions
4　Dreams
5　Words of Wisdom
6　Understanding
7　Revelation Knowledge
8　Tongues and Interpretation of Tongues
9　Prophecy

Michael Janiczek

Chapter Four

My Ears Were Opened

There I was, driving my car at 2:00 AM. I had just been through one of the most amazing church services in my life, our ordination ceremony, when suddenly God began to speak to me.

As I said before, Karen and I went to Bible College together at New Life Bible College in Cleveland, Tennessee. We graduated in 1978. We decided at that time to wait to be ordained. We felt led instead to be lay ministers in our church. So after Bible College, we moved back to Chicago, found jobs and continued to work as volunteers at our church.

Over the years we worked at various churches, first in youth and young adult ministries, then as home group leaders for young married couples. I also taught the Bible at church and in home groups whenever the opportunity arose.

Karen worked in Children's Church ministry, which involved a puppet team as well as writing and producing a weekly soap opera type story for kids' church. The main characters in her weekly drama were named Peggy Sue and George. Karen played the part of

Peggy Sue and a friend of ours named John Dillon played her older brother George. This weekly children's church drama combined biblical stories with everyday life for the kids. Karen is a brilliant leader and an awesome writer. She created weekly skits for many years. The children in that church could not wait to come to church each week to see what would happen next.

The interesting thing was that Karen was then in her thirties, playing an 8-year-old girl, and George was in his forties, playing a 10-year-old boy. The children were captivated by their weekly adventures - so much so that they really believed that Peggy Sue and George were children who were brother and sister.

One day Karen and I were in a grocery store when a young girl approached Karen and asked her where her brother George was. The child then turned to me and asked if I was her (Peggy Sue's) daddy. She actually believed Karen was Peggy Sue and George was her brother. She saw Karen as an 8-year- old, but looking at me she saw an older adult who she assumed was Peggy Sue's daddy. I was amazed at the impact Karen had on those children during that time of her ministry.

As for me, I played trumpet in the 20-piece church orchestra. This was not an ordinary group of volunteer musicians, as most were professional players. I became a leader in the group and headed the "home group" that consisted of orchestra members. We played at church during every service, which included three services on Sunday mornings, one on Sunday night as well as

Wednesday evening service. Needless to say, we stayed very busy, as this was volunteer work. Karen was at home during the week raising our children, while I had a full time job in sales and marketing.

Over the years we discussed getting ordained but until recently we never had felt led to do it. Part of our ministry each year was to produce and direct musicals around two major church events each year, Christmas and Easter. We decided to try putting on a Christian production outside of the church. Therefore we formed a new non-profit ministry called Dreamstone Productions that would serve as a Para-church ministry producing musicals and dramas in the local theaters.

We would do these productions by working with local churches in an area that would provide talent, support and funding in their local community. We felt that getting ordained would give us a needed legitimacy, as some of these pastors did not know who we were.

So there I was driving home from the ordination service when God began to speak to me. He told me He was well pleased with both Karen and me, and He wanted me to know that this was just the beginning of what He had planned for us. I began to cry.

In the car with me were Karen and two of our three children, Heather and David. They were all concerned to see me openly crying like that. I do not think they ever had seen me cry before. I was like a blubbering idiot trying to explain that everything was all right and that God was speaking to me. I do not know what they thought, but they did let me be, as God continued to bless me and show me things that evening. It was just the beginning.

The next morning Karen, and David and myself were in the middle of our daily prayer time when the Spirit of God came all over me and began to show me some amazing things. I was having an open vision!

All of a sudden, I saw God followed by a column of angels heading towards my home, into our back yard. When they got right in front of me, God said He was bringing us a special blessing! As He stepped aside, I saw this column of angels lined up two-by- two coming towards us.

They each had a large container full of oil, and as they came before me, my wife and son, they poured it on and into us. As the oil covered and consumed us, I had a feeling of warmth and exhilaration come over me. While some of the oil was covering us, I realized that most of it was being poured into me, my wife and son. This went on for quite some time as angels kept appearing before us.

When it was over I had a feeling of peace and rest all over my body. I then asked God what this was and He said, "It is restoration oil." He said, "Whenever you or anyone around you feels weak and stressed out and you need restoration in your body, just call on this oil of restoration and you will be restored." He said, "I have given you more than enough, so that you will never need."

At that point I opened my eyes and I was sitting there in my home praying with my wife. I shared with her what I had seen and we rejoiced together.

There have been times in my life since then when I realized that I needed that restoration oil, and every time I call on it, it bathes me in its warmth and I am completely restored. We have also prayed for others to receive it and they have felt it as well!

We were at a meeting with two of our friends who are prophets and we were all ministering. Shawn Patrick Williams came to my wife and said he was finished ministering. He was exhausted and was going to sit down. She said she wanted him to pray for another person, and he said he had nothing. So she laid her hands on him and prayed for the restoration oil she was given, and when she was done, Shawn was amazed at the strength and clarity he received and went back to ministering to people. Later he commented on how "done" he was and had nothing more to give and then, when Karen prayed for him, he was restored.

I give God all of the glory for this amazing gift He gave to me and to Karen.

Ongoing Communication or Something New?

Now that the lines of communication are opened, I have had an ongoing conversation with God. My prayer life has gone from a once in a while occurrence, that was usually motivated by an important need or terrible tragedy that had already occurred, to a daily prayer time where I talk with God and tell Him what I need as well as what I want.

> *²⁴Therefore I say unto you, What things so ever ye desire, when ye pray, believe that ye receive them, and ye shall have them.*
> *(Mark 11:24)*

God wants to give us the desires of our heart.

Imagine if Bill Gates offered you a blank check for you to pay off your house, your car and all of your bills, plus a few million dollars extra to set you up for life. Wouldn't that be great?

God said whatsoever things you desire when you pray, believe you have them and you shall receive them. It is just like getting a blank check every day.

Why would God make such an offer? He does it because He loves us and because He wants to provide us with what we need to fulfill the great commission.

Chapter Five

He Was There All The Time

I am convinced that God did not change, I did. It was a change in my life that resulted in my ears being opened to hear God. After all, my wife had been praying for this to happen for many years. I had to decide to make the effort to get closer to God to be able to hear Him. Yes, He helped me along the way and moved on others to pray both for me and with me, but I had to come to the realization that I was away from God and had to make a move closer to Him for this to happen.

Why am I so sure? Here is what the Bible says:

[8]Jesus Christ the same yesterday, and to day, and for ever. (Hebrews 13:8)

[34]Then Peter opened his mouth, and said, Of a truth I perceive that God is no respecter of persons: (Acts 10:34)

Since He is the same yesterday, today and forever and is no respecter of persons, it would be incorrect to believe that God changed in any way so that I could get closer to Him. God does not change for us to get to know Him; we change in order to get closer to Him.

It took a change in the way I acted, a conversion in my heart and a change in my actions to bring me closer to Him - close enough to hear His voice. I believe that He desires constant communication with us, but we are not engaging Him.

Communication is the key!

God is very logical. All relationships that we have in life are centered on one important thing: communication. Why would we think a relationship with Him would require anything else? The Bible says:

> [9]*And I say unto you, Ask, and it shall be given you; seek, and ye shall find; knock, and it shall be opened unto you.. (Luke 11:9)*

I had heard and read that scripture many times, but I did not totally understand it. Now I get it. If I will seek communication with Him, He will respond. Ii is a two-way street that requires me to engage Him. Since He is no respecter of persons, He cannot and will not do for me something that He would not do for you. Therefore, I am convinced that you can have the same level of communication with God that I have. Just start communicating with Him. It is that simple!

Prayer is the way we communicate with God. All my life, prayer seemed like a chore. I was born and raised Catholic, and the two repetitive prayers that we were taught to recite had no meaning to me as a child. Then when I grew up and became born again, I did not know how to pray.

Yes, I said the sinner's prayer. Yes, I learned how to give thanks and pray for my meals. Yes, I learned how to pray for others while in Bible College. Yes, I knew I should pray every day, but I never learned how to do it. At times in my life I would get real with a pastor or friend and admit that I knew that I was lacking a productive prayer life. No one seemed to be able to tell me what to do to establish my prayer life, the how-to direction that I needed.

What finally ended up happening was that I started having daily encounters with God

Not only that, but now that I know how God communicates, I realize that He was there all the time. Many times in the past I heard Him, but not only did I not know it was He, I did not listen to what He had to say.

I found out that as the Bible says in, Hebrews 4:12 *"the word of God is quick, and powerful, and sharper than any two-edged sword . . ."* He usually speaks a few words, but when you listen to those words, their meaning speaks volumes. It is like a hyperlink on a computer. The link can be a short sentence or even one or two words, but when you click on it, it expands into volumes of information. That is what God's Word is like. One short verse expands into volumes of meaning when you pursue it.

Chapter Six

He Talks To Me
Every Day
In Various Ways

Once my ears were opened, I began to realize that God speaks to me in various ways.

We have already covered the fact that God is a rewarder of those who diligently seek Him, so keeping that in mind; I began to consider the gifts of the Spirit, which God says are available to believers who seek them.

The nine gifts of the Spirit are recorded in 1 Corinthians, Chapter 12.

[7]But the manifestation of the Spirit is given to every man to profit withal. [8]For to one is given by the Spirit the word of wisdom; to another the word of knowledge by the same Spirit; [9]To another faith by the same Spirit; to another the gifts of healing by the same Spirit; [10]To another the working of miracles; to another

> *prophecy; to another discerning of spirits; to another divers kinds of tongues; to another the interpretation of tongues:* [11]*But all these worketh that one and the selfsame Spirit, dividing to every man severally as he will. (1Cor 12:7-11)*

The gifts can be categorized in three groups as follows:

1 **Power Gifts:**
   Miracles
   Healing
   Special Faith

2) **Revelation Gifts:**
   Word of Wisdom
   Word of Knowledge
   Discerning of Spirits

3) **Vocal Gifts:**
   Tongues
   Interpretation of Tongues
   Prophecy

Knowing that God wants to give us these gifts and that He is a rewarder of those who diligently seek Him, I ask Him every day for wisdom, understanding and revelation knowledge; for divine health for me and my family, and for whatever gift He wants me to have today.

I also make professions of faith regarding my family and their salvation. I confess that as for me and my house, we will serve the Lord.

I profess and proclaim that my business prospers; that I am a leader in my field. And that I am blessed when I enter a room and blessed when I leave a room, and whatsoever things I do shall prosper. That no weapon formed against me shall prosper. That I prosper and am in health even as my soul prospers.

We tear down the strongholds that the enemy has planted in our lives. We break every curse that has been spoken against us, or any curse we have spoken over ourselves or any generational curse that has been handed down to us that we do not even know of.

Since we have been praying this way, we have seen strongholds broken in our lives. We identified these as a spirit of poverty and a spirit of un-forgiveness.

The effect of having a spirit of poverty was that no matter how much money we made in a year, we never had anything left over. We did not spend frivolously, we did not go on trips, buy expensive cars or live extravagantly, but we never had any extra money. Something would always come up and cost us everything we had saved. Through prayer and confession, God removed this spirit from us and we now prosper in business and regularly save.

Second, God helped us to recognize that we were harboring un-forgiveness. We had not completely forgiven those who had done us wrong over the years. When this realization came, we immediately confessed our fault and asked for forgiveness ourselves, and that spirit was lifted off of me.

Ever since I have been asking, I have been receiving. Every day I ask for wisdom, understanding and revelation knowledge. By definition, here is what I am asking for:

Wisdom is the quality or state of being wise; knowledge of what is true or right, coupled with just judgment as to action; discernment, or insight.

Understanding is the mental process of a person who comprehends a superior power of discernment; enlightened intelligence. Also expanded knowledge or familiarity with a particular thing, skill in dealing with or handling something.

Revelation knowledge is the act of revealing or disclosing facts, truths, or principles of *many things.*

He has given all of this to me. I also confess and proclaim the good things that God says in His Word that we have.

We proclaim that we walk in divine health.

We profess that we are blessed and highly favored

Sometimes I get a word of wisdom or a word of knowledge where all of a sudden I know something that

I must do or that I did not know before. Sometimes it is in an open vision or dream while I am sleeping. (I have had visions while in prayer and dreams in the night while I was sleeping when God has spoken to me). Sometimes it comes through the words of a Christian song I am singing or while I am watching television or a movie. Sometimes it comes when I am cutting the lawn or driving the car.

I cannot say that every time God speaks to me I actually hear His voice. That has happened. However, it is not always audible. Sometimes He plants thoughts in my mind. Sometimes He shows me something and then I get the understanding. Sometimes I get a vision or what I call a flash vision where I see something very quickly and then get the meaning. However or wherever He speaks, it usually points me to a scripture verse in the Bible or a biblical truth that He is trying to teach me.

I find His words to me are always edifying, exhortative, corrective, confirming or comforting words. They give me function, purpose and direction for my life, family and business. They always bring me peace, even when they are correction.

Michael Janiczek

Suggested Prayers

Since God created us to have fellowship with Him, we need to communicate with Him every day. How do you do that? Through prayer.

A good friend of mine, Pastor Forson Swanzy, worked with me to put together these prayers. My wife and I used them during our daily devotions for several weeks to declare and decree the good things that God had in store for us. We used them as a guide that in essence taught us how to communicate (pray) with God every day.

If you are like I was, not knowing how to pray, I recommend that you start by using these prayers as a daily guide.

As was the case with us, I believe that over time you will learn to rely less and less on these pre-written prayers and begin to communicate (pray) directly with God from your heart.

These prayers are designated for specific needs as follows:

Deliverance
I believe and confess that the Lord is good, for I am delivered from the traps of the enemy. The Son of

God sets me free and I am free indeed. No evil befalls me. No weapon formed against me shall prosper.

I apply the armor of God to my life. Every fiery dart of Satan falls at my feet, for the shield of faith protects me. Any bondage of the devil is cancelled, in Jesus' Name, for I am out of bondage and into liberty. I break and cancel any and all curses over my life: curses that I may have spoken, curses others have spoken over me or any generational curse from my forefathers. I break them all, in Jesus' Name. Furthermore, I replace all curses with blessings, and I command Satan to return, replace and restore anything that has been stolen from me, in Jesus' Name.

Christ has redeemed me from the curse of the law. I am free from the power of the evil one. My freedom is guaranteed in Jesus. I am covered by His precious blood.

I am blessed and highly favored. I confess, proclaim and decree that I am blessed, my family is blessed, my business is blessed, my work is blessed, and that whatsoever things I do shall prosper, in Jesus' Name.

Difficult People

I believe and confess that God is good. His faithfulness extends to the heavens. I give God praise because He gives me wisdom to handle people who are difficult. I bless the Name of the Lord for giving me victory over every satanic lie.

I confess by faith that the dishonest are exposed and that those who mean evil against my life are revealed by the Holy Spirit. I am free from the fear of man. I am victorious over impossible people. I reject the works of the enemy and confess that I have received wisdom to handle those who make unnecessary demands on my life. I have received wisdom to deal with the difficult, for the Spirit of the Lord anoints my eyes to see the false as well as the truthful.

My eyes are anointed to see the plans of the enemy. My heart is filled with wisdom to handle every situation. No evil, danger or weapon formed against me prospers, for the Lord exposes everyone who would betray me; those who belittle me shall see me make progress.

The blood of Jesus covers me against every critical spirit, against every spirit of jealousy and against every conspirator who is against me. By faith I confess that I am victorious in every situation, and everything I touch and do will carry the mark of God's blessing. I am blessed and highly favored, in Jesus' Name.

Divine Elevation

I believe and confess that the favor of the Lord is on my life. The steadfast love of the Lord never fails.

He loves me and lifts me out of the dust of defeat. He has brought me into a place of promotion.

By faith I confess that the cycle of degradation and defeat is broken in my life, for the Lord has made me sit in the heavenly places with Him. My promotion is of the Lord and not from man. I confess boldly that every pit that the enemy has dug for my life will become a steppingstone to a higher level for me.

I confess that the prosperity of God rests upon my life, for the Lord makes room for me and increases my capacity. The testimony of the Lord in my life is one of promotion - the kind of promotion that will take me from prison to palace. I receive the divine endorsement of the Lord on everything I do. I believe and confess that deeper knowledge of the Lord and wisdom from above flow in my life.

No temptation shall pull me down, for the Lord Himself promotes me and lifts my head in the midst of adversity to possess the land. I confess boldly that the horn of my strength shall be exalted and the grace of God shall abound in my life for all eyes to see. I boldly confess that I have come out of sadness into God's joy. I am blessed and highly favored.

Divine Favor

I believe and confess that God's plan is to prosper me and not to harm me. God's plan is to elevate me, for eye has not seen, ear has not heard, nor has it come into our understanding what God still has in store for me. For the Lord is giving me joy in all things, causing favor and blessing to flow in my life. The favor of the Lord goes with me everywhere and the Lord's blessing is manifest even in adverse situations. God's favor to collect the wealth of the wicked rests upon me. God's divine elevation in the sight of the enemy rests upon my life. The grace of the Lord goes with me and causes me to stand before kings and to have favor with all men.

The favor of the Lord brings notice to my life in the presence of those who will bless and promote me. God's grace and favor and honor rest on my life and will frustrate the enemy. The favor of the Lord, which brings me wisdom, understanding and knowledge, is continually coming my way. I am receiving new ideas and am favored with new understanding. I believe and confess that I will be patient until the day of my promotion.

I confess that the kindness of the Lord is upon my life and extends to the heavens. God satisfies my mouth with good things. He takes my mourning and gives me laughter. My weeping may have been for a night, but now my joy has come forth. The favor of God's anointing and strength is upon my life. It flows in me and causes me to rise above all situations. The favor that follows a wise servant is upon my life. I am blessed and highly favored.

Dominion

I believe and confess that the Lord is good. I praise God for giving me the victory and dominion over the challenges of life. I boldly confess that God causes me to break all evil dominion of the enemy over my life and to exercise godly dominion over everything around me, in the Name of Jesus.

According to God's Word, I have dominion over every situation in my life. I declare that anything that rises up against me will come under my authority, in the name of Jesus. Death has no power over me, for the Lord, who is mightier than my enemies, is dwelling in me. I confess that I will reach my destined position as ordained by the Lord. The enemy will not triumph over any area of my life. I exercise the authority and dominion that belong to the upright, in Jesus' Name.

I boldly declare my dominion in all situations. I have dominion over the challenges that have troubled my mind. I have victory over sickness, disease and death, regardless of my immediate circumstances. I forbid sickness and disease to have any effect on my body, in the Name of Jesus. I exercise dominion over every spirit that tries to break the peace of God in my body, in my mind, in my family, in my life and in my home. I thank the Lord for the power to loose on earth all that has been granted me by heaven.

I boldly declare that every generational curse that might hinder my flow in Christ is nullified, in the Name of Jesus, and I declare that every spirit contrary to the Spirit of Christ is under subjection, or God gives me victory, favor and dominion. I am blessed and highly favored.

Faithfulness of God

I believe and confess that the Lord is good. I thank the Lord for His faithfulness at all times in my life. The faithfulness of the Lord is known to me as I face the challenges of life. God will not fail me for He is a covenant-keeping God. His faithfulness makes guidance available to me, even in what appears to be my darkest hour. His faithfulness will make Him finish what He started in my life, for His Word says in Philippians 1:6 *"And I am convinced and sure of this very thing, that He Who began a good work in me will continue until the day of Jesus Christ [right up to the time of His return], developing [that good work] and perfecting and bringing it to full completion in me."* *(Ampl.)*

The Lord is more than enough for me, and I trust Him even to the ends of the earth. I am blessed and highly favored.

Family

I believe and confess that God is good. I thank the Lord for His faithfulness to my family. I receive the grace of God to maintain unity and love in my marriage.

No weapon formed against my home shall prosper. I take authority over every demonic assignment set up against me, my marriage, my family and/or my relationships. And I command all evil forces to leave me, in Jesus' Name. The spirit of jealousy is bound from coming near me or my home. My family and I are covered with the blood of Jesus; my home shall be a place of divine order.

I give God glory because He delivers me and my family from all evil. I am blessed and highly favored.

Fear

I believe and confess that I have victory over the challenges of life, for the Lord has promised not to leave me or forsake me. I receive boldness instead of fear to face the challenges.

I boldly declare that the weapons of the enemy shall have no effect on me. I know that fear is a spirit for God's Word tells me in 2 Timothy 1:7, *"For God hath not given us the spirit of fear; but of power, and of love, and of a sound mind."* Therefore, since He has not given me the spirit of fear, I reject the interference of the spirit of fear in my life. I reject any and all fears, and I break every tormenting effect which fear has had over my life.

I declare that all news contrary to my joy shall be turned around. I receive God's grace to trust Him without doubt. I am blessed and highly favored.

Finances

I believe and confess that the Lord is good. He is faithful to all those who trust in Him.

I give God praise for providing increase in my life. I rejoice because the Lord has brought to my life blessings that make me rich. He has given me the seeds of finances to minister to others who lack. This is my day of harvest.

This is my time of increase. God has a storehouse in heaven full of everything I will ever need. His Word proclaims in John 1:3, *"All things were made by him; and without him was not any thing made that was made."* Therefore I know that God already has provided anything and everything that I will ever need.

Through God I declare my freedom from the shackles of debt. I worship the Lord, Who owns the cattle upon a thousand hills. I give Him praise for making me a partaker of the transfer of wealth from the wicked to the righteous. I am financially buoyant in Christ, enjoying His increase every day. I am blessed and highly favored.

Focus

I give God praise for the wondrous works He is doing in my life. I thank God because He is the author and finisher of my faith. I boldly reject every form of satanic destruction aimed at me and I break free from them in Jesus' Name.

I know that God created me for a specific purpose and to carry out a specific plan. He reveals His plans to me and I confess that I am equipped and anointed to carry out my destiny in God. Therefore, I reject every time-wasting dream and every tendency to jealousy over other people's gifts that would try to overtake me. The grace of the Lord abounds on my life and opens me to the gifting deposited in me.

I shall possess my possession and see the fulfillment of my vision. My eyes are on my breakthrough despite any report to the contrary. I break free from any ungodly habit that might hold me back. I am blessed and highly favored.

Forgiveness

I believe and confess that the Lord is good and His mercy endures forever. The Lord has changed my mourning into dancing, for He has cleansed me from all unrighteousness and sin.

I believe and confess that the riches of God's grace abound upon me and help me to forgive those who have offended me.

God fills me with unconditional love, so I refuse to live with offense against other people. I choose to bless and not to curse. I choose to wish good to people, and not evil. I have found that I have the ability to live in peace, for I am filled with the love of God. The Lord has redeemed my life from destruction and set my feet on the solid Rock. I am blessed and highly favored.

Freedom from Bondage

I give God praise for freedom, which He has given me in the Holy Spirit. I thank the Lord for He has made me totally victorious over every binding spirit. In the Name of the Lord Jesus, I am free from the bondage of depression, I am free from the tendency to a spirit of desperation, and my heart is free from a faultfinding spirit. I am not defeated.

I am filled with the spirit of boldness. I overcome every tendency that is contrary to the presence of the Holy Spirit. I am a child of God and He gives me victory over every doubting spirit, unhealthy competitiveness, and the tendency to be blindly aggressive.

By faith I confess that the blood of Jesus works in my life against every seductive spirit and sets me totally free from every snare of the enemy.

I confess that I am free from the spirit of unhappiness and depression. The Spirit of the Lord breaks me free from the feeling of worthlessness. I am totally free from every tendency to be unstable. By faith I confess that the Holy Spirit has given me victory in every area of my life and I am growing in the grace of Jesus Christ, overcoming daily by the Spirit and the Word.

I am not a slave to any form of bondage, but totally free in Jesus Christ. I am blessed and highly favored.

Fruitfulness

I believe and confess that the Lord is good; He causes me to have victory at all times and in every circumstance. Through Him, fruitfulness follows everything I do. Because I am the planting of the Lord, fruitfulness follows wherever I am. The grace of the Lord delivers me from spiritual barrenness; and He brings fruitfulness in every area where there has been barrenness in my life, in the Name of Jesus. I am increasing every day in my fruit bearing.

I boldly confess that increase follows everything I do. I shall still bear fruit that brings glory to God in old age. I shall bear the fruit of patience in my life, in the name of Jesus. By faith, I command that any barrenness in my life will break forth into fruitfulness. I shall see my children's children and blessings in all that I do.

The Lord will turn the place of my enslavement into a place of fruitfulness. The Lord will transform my life from one degree of fruitfulness to a greater one.

I confess by faith the blessings of the Lord on the labor of my hands. I declare that I prosper through the initiatives I am involved in and, even in my trying times, fruit will follow my effort. I shall have reasons to praise God at all times for I shall see the fruit of my lips created. I am blessed and highly favored.

The Future

I bless the Name of the Lord for His daily leading. I thank Him for not withholding any good thing from me because I trust Him.

I boldly confess that all things will work together for my good because I love the Lord. The future of my marriage is secure in the Lord. The future of my children is secure in the Lord. My future will portray God's manifest blessing.

I boldly confess that the Lord is my Shepherd; therefore I shall not miss fulfilling my purpose. The Lord has built His hedge around me to give me protection and guarantee my future. Everything I lay my hand to shall be accomplished, for the Lord causes success to attend all that I do. I am blessed and highly favored.

Growth

I believe and confess that the Lord is good. Every good Word of the Lord in my life shall bring forth fruit.

I boldly declare that I have received grace to grow in my relationship with Him. The seed of God's Word will fall on good ground in my life.

By faith I confess that I have received grace to walk with God and to understand His Word. His Word bears fruit in my life, for the success of the Lord attends all I do.

I boldly declare that I receive grace to put away immature behavior and to grow more in the Lord. My eyes are open to the deeper things of God, so that I increase in the knowledge of the Lord. I soar above all situations like an eagle, experiencing growth and increase in every area. I am blessed and highly favored.

Guidance

I believe and confess that the Lord is good. I rejoice before Him with gratitude for His daily leading. The Spirit of the Lord is my guide through the darkness of this world. He orders my steps so that I do not fear.

I boldly confess that my confidence is in the Lord and not in any earthly guide. He leads me and shows me the way. The hand of the Lord shall lead me in my career. My steps are ordered to the place of fruitfulness. I receive the anointing of the Holy Spirit for every endeavor I embark on. He will lead me to accomplish what I have begun. I am blessed and highly favored.

Healing

I believe and confess that the Lord is good. He is faithful at all times to keep His Word. God will not withhold any good thing from those who love Him. I give praise to the Lord for His work of healing in my life.

I take authority over every affliction and destroy the impact of sickness. I command diseases in the bone to die. I curse every impurity of the blood. I take authority over every disease of the heart and receive healing, in the Name of Jesus. Cancer and other destructive diseases have no power over me, for the Lord God is my Jehovah Rapha, my Healer. He remembers my tears of affliction and takes away tears from members of my household.

I believe and confess that I have inner healing for ailments I cannot see. Every satanic virus is cursed at the root. Affliction is not my portion. I reject every problem of blood disease and receive healing for every area of my life.

I boldly confess that I am anointed to bring healing to masses of people. The Lord shall deliver those in bondage through me. The ministry of healing shall flow forth through me, in the Name of Jesus, for I am blessed and highly favored.

Hunger for Righteousness

I believe and confess that the grace of God is sufficient for me. I have been delivered from the power and penalty of sin.

I boldly declare that everything I am and have is for the kingdom of God. My heart is yielded to do the will of God. His love fills my heart. I am anointed to operate in holy zeal.

I boldly declare that the grace of God will help me to be faithful to the end, to walk in righteousness all of my life.

I receive boldness to break free from bondages, to endure persecution. I boldly declare that the voice of the Holy Spirit will lead me, and my hunger to fulfill His purpose shall increase. I am blessed and highly favored.

Increase

I believe and confess that the Lord is faithful at all times. I praise Him for causing me to be favored of men and for favoring me Himself.

I boldly confess that my eyes are anointed to discover and enjoy the favor of the Lord.

I confess the blessings of God on my business, and on everything I put my hands to do. Supernatural breakthrough follows me. I am experiencing God's abundant increase. I am anointed to experience multiple increases. Barrenness is over, in Jesus' Name. I shall increase in spiritual understanding. There shall be great increase in blessing, and favor. The days of my small beginnings are turning into a time of great abundance. I am blessed and highly favored.

Knowledge
The knowledge of the Lord is pleasant to my soul, and causes me to increase in everything I do. By faith I receive the ability to operate in divine knowledge.

I boldly confess that I have insight from God into people's real problems. The knowledge of the Lord helps me to bring solutions to people's challenges and lives. I am a blessing to my generation. I boldly confess that through me words of excellence and wisdom will flow. The words that proceed from me will bless those who come in contact with me.

I believe and confess that I have received the anointing to operate in supernatural knowledge. The treasures of wisdom and knowledge are residing in me. Through God, I have the grace to walk in His wisdom. I am blessed and highly favored.

Security
I boldly confess and give God praise for being my refuge and strength in the time of trouble. I thank the Lord for He is my defense against the enemy's attack. The Lord will cause me to know His arm of protection at all times and He will cause me to learn to put my trust in Him. I dwell in the land of safety, by faith, and no one or nothing shall make me afraid. I confess that the Holy Spirit will build and fortify His hedge around me. I am surrounded with the

peace of God and I take authority over every trouble that would cause me to fret.

By faith I confess that no weapon of the enemy formed against me prospers and every tongue that rises against me in judgment is condemned. The angel of the Lord will scatter all those who are plotting against me. The Lord Himself shall uphold me with His mighty power.

The Name of the Lord has become my dwelling place. He lifts my head above that of the enemy and gives me authority over every demonic force that may be attacking me.

I boldly declare victory over the terror of the night and the evil of darkness. I cover myself from the pestilence of the enemy that would envelop me. I release angelic presence around my home in the Name of the Lord to watch over me, guide me, protect me and minister to me as needed, in Jesus' Name. I am blessed and highly favored.

Self-Esteem

I bless the Name of the Lord. I thank my Lord and Savior Jesus Christ for setting me free from the power and bondage of insecurity. I give God praise because every evil pronouncement made into my life must turn around in my favor.

I break the power of emotional bondage and I loose myself from the control of the evil one. I declare myself totally free from the bondage of selfishness, self-righteousness and self-pity. By faith I declare that every spirit of self-abuse and self-pity is gone from me in Jesus' Name. I boldly declare that God uses me for His glory, for I am His new creation, created in Christ Jesus for His glory and for His praise.

I confess boldly that I walk in Christ, I live in Christ and I am growing in the grace of Jesus Christ. I am motivated daily to be an achiever. I am finding my value in God for I am bought with a high price. According to His Word He has sealed me with His Holy Spirit of promise.

This means that I have been inspected and approved by God to carry out my destiny in Him. The blood of Jesus cleanses me from all unrighteousness. Therefore I have victory in the Lord Jesus Christ. He has given me dominion over every challenge that I may face. I am blessed and highly favored.

Serving the Lord

I give God the praise for making me a minister of the gospel for His glory. I thank the Lord for the boldness to preach His Word, even in the most adverse situations. I thank the Lord for strengthening me to be able to serve Him.

I boldly confess that the power of God, the blood of Jesus and the power and anointing of the Holy Spirit will be manifested in me and in my ministry and that the Lord will confirm His Word as I speak it.

Like Joseph with Potiphar, serving my Master well will open the doors of grace and favor for me. I receive by faith divine approval upon my ministry in the Name of Jesus.

I believe and confess that the Lord gives me the strength to commit myself totally to His purpose and counsel. I confess that I shall not serve money, but that I will serve the Lord, for the Lord will reward my service in the name of Jesus. I give God the praise for the heart of a servant that dwells in me. I thank the Lord for the ability to serve Him with a heart of humility. I boldly confess that the Lord strengthens me to serve Him, even in the most difficult circumstances. I am blessed and highly favored.

Strength

I believe and confess that the Lord is good. He causes me to be strengthened day-to-day, for the Lord is making my life a wall of strength in the land. God causes my life to be like an iron pillar and a brazen wall. Even my weak moments reveal the power of God. The ability of God to transform my weakness into strength flows in my life.

I boldly confess the grace to be fruitful in my walk with the Lord, for God causes me to increase in the knowledge of Him. The Lord strengthens me with all His might.

By faith I prevail with God in prayer. I confess that God becomes my strength and help in the time of need, and the power of God in my life will mark His calling on my life. I release the strength of the Lord against any impossible situation I am facing and receive divine breakthrough as I confront every challenge.

I boldly declare that the anointing to counter the onslaught of the enemy rests upon me. I confess by faith that irrespective of what I see, His strength shall match my days on earth. The Lord will always be my source of strength. The divine intervention of God in what I am facing will follow at all times, in Jesus' Name.

I boldly declare that God becomes my source of deliverance and causes me to rise above every situation. The nets and traps of the enemy are broken for my sake; the oppression of the enemy is shattered for my sake. I come under the shelter of the Almighty God during the attacks of the enemy.

I take refuge under His strength. He becomes my help in my time of need and He will always be there whenever I am faced with challenges. I am blessed and highly favored.

Triumph

I boldly sing to the Lord a song of triumph for His victory over my enemies. I give God praise for helping me to overcome the lies of the devil. I thank my Lord and Savior for His faithfulness to deliver His children from the aggression of the enemy. The Lord makes a way for me out of every difficult situation.

By faith I confess that I escape every situation set by the enemy, for the Lord will frustrate the plans of evildoers and He will cause every journey of the enemy to end in his own pit.

I boldly confess that the oppressor and his weapons will drown in his own Red Sea. I declare by faith that the children of evildoers shall not overcome me; rather I shall be triumphant in all that I lay my hands upon.

By faith I confess that the enemy shall have no reason to rejoice over me, for the Lord will counter every evil imagination of Satan against my life and my home.

I believe and confess that I receive breakthrough that will cause a triumphant shout in the house of God on my behalf. I give God praise for causing me to be triumphant at all times over the works of Satan, over the attacks of the enemy and over the lies spoken against me.

I boldly confess that the Lord will make a public show of the victory He is bringing into my life. I boldly command the fury of the Lord to come upon the enemy that seeks my destruction. I declare that I tread upon the enemy and He is under my feet. I thank the Lord for His promise to put the enemy under my feet at all times and to give me victory over everything that rises against me.

My trust is in the Lord and not in my weapons. Therefore I take authority over every serpentine spirit and declare total victory in the Name of Jesus. I am blessed and highly favored.

Trust

I believe and confess that the Lord has given me the grace and privilege of knowing Him. My heart trusts in the Lord for He has promised to be my help in time of need.

I boldly confess that my trust is in the Lord; therefore I shall not lack anything. Fear has no hold over my life. The weapon of discouragement is cancelled, in the Name of Jesus. Each day of my life shall reveal His glory. Because I trust in the Lord, I shall be like Mount Zion, which cannot be moved. I am blessed and highly favored.

Unity

I believe and confess that the Lord is good. His faithfulness is forever more. I give praise to the Lord for unity in our church, in my marriage and at work.

I boldly confess that I walk in love, and I receive the grace that guards the unity of the body of Christ. The spirits of division, hatred and selfishness are far from me. I leave no room for discord. I give God praise for giving me victory in Jesus Christ. I am blessed and highly favored.

Vision

I believe and confess that God gives me the vision necessary to make me progress in life. I thank the Lord for His vision and will for my life. I boldly confess that my eyes are anointed to see God's plan for the future. God gives me insight into my destiny. The eyes of my understanding are enlightened; the purpose of my calling is made clear and known unto me.

I boldly confess that I will pursue the vision of my life, whether others believe in it or not. I boldly confess that the Lord will send people who will understand and believe my vision and He will give me a heart to pursue the purpose for which I have been created.

I believe and confess that I fully understand my God-given vision and I progress in it no matter its size. Everything that comes against my vision shall fall for my sake, for the Lord will cause an explosion of the gift of revelation in the midst of my troubles.

By faith I confess a heart of humility regarding the great visions that the Lord shows me. I receive clear and divine understanding for life. The Lord Himself will cause me to have a clearly defined destination. He shall be my help to carry out His plan for my life.

I receive the anointing of the Holy Spirit to carry out the vision of God for my life. In all circumstances, I give God praise in advance for giving me fulfillment in every aspect of life. I am blessed and highly favored.

Winning

I believe and confess that God is good, for He causes me to have victory through the Lord Jesus Christ. I thank the Lord for defeating Satan on my behalf in the name of Jesus. By faith I confess that the power of the Lord will prevail over the challenges that I am facing.

I confess that the hand of the enemy will not prevail against me. Rather, through every weariness, tiredness and attack of the enemy; I gain victory in the Name of Jesus.

By faith I confess that I will succeed in spite of many failures, for the Lord will make my life peculiar to Him out of many people. God will cause me to have victory over sin and dominion over situations. By faith I confess that I will eat the good of the land. I give God praise for turning around famine years and making them harvest times. I bless the Name of the Lord because He will bring an abundant harvest as I sow the seed I have.

I praise the Name of the Lord because He will destroy every attack of Satan. I do not lean on my own understanding, but totally depend on the grace of God. Every project I lay my hand to will succeed.

The Lord will cause every demonic onslaught to be defeated for my sake. The devil will not prevail over my life or anything that belongs to me. The Word of God is the basis for my success and He will link me with those who will bless me.

I have victory over every problem and situation. The Lord strengthens my hands, and the voice of victory shall never be stopped in my household. The favor and the blessing of the Lord rest upon my home, for the hand of opposition shall fail against me. The Lord will raise me up and make me a testimony of His wealth and riches, to the glory of His Name. I am blessed and highly favored.

Work

I give God the praise for the opportunity to be alive and healthy today. I thank the Lord for access to His throne through the Lord Jesus Christ. I bless the Name of the Lord for proving Himself mighty and strong on my behalf. By faith I confess that the Lord gives me opportunities to touch humanity with my talent.

I am a blessing to the human race. I take authority over the spirit of disunity and betrayal that would find a way into work, in the Name of Jesus. No evil befalls me and no danger comes near my working or dwelling place. He will cause me to shine as light in this crooked world.

I thank the Lord in advance, for my labor will not be in vain. God Himself will show His blessing and favor upon me and command fruitfulness on every venture I carry out. I take authority over sickness that tries to hinder me from achieving my vision. I subdue hindrances to my business or work and cancel all such hindrance, in the name of Jesus. I receive breakthrough in the area of my finances in the Name of Jesus.

I bless the Name of the Lord because He causes me to increase. All that I have is covered with the blood of Jesus. I give God praise for His faithfulness. I am blessed and highly favored.

Mike Janiczek is available for speaking engagements and personal appearances. For more information contact:

Mike Janiczek
C/O Advantage Books
P.O. Box 160847
Altamonte Springs, Florida 32716

To purchase additional copies of this book or other books published by Advantage Books call our toll free order number at:
1-888-383-3110 (Book Orders Only)

or visit our bookstore website at:
www.advbookstore.com

Longwood, Florida, USA
"we bring dreams to life"™
www.advbooks.com

Printed in the United States
153384LV00001B/6/P